P35-36

ERNEST KEVAN

Pastor and Principal

ERNEST KEVAN

Pastor and Principal

by

GILBERT W. KIRBY

VICTORY PRESS

LONDON AND EASTBOURNE

SBN 85476 001 6

Printed in Great Britain for
VICTORY PRESS (Evangelical Publishers Ltd)
Lottbridge Drove, Eastbourne, Sussex, by
Richard Clay (The Chaucer Press), Ltd.,
Bungay, Suffolk.

FOREWORD

That Dr. Kevan's successor as Principal of the London Bible College should take it upon himself to write his biography calls for a word of explanation. While to undertake such an assignment constitutes a rare privilege, it is one from which I naturally shrink. In the first place, the subject is one who is worthy of far more detailed consideration than such a slim volume allows. Furthermore, the writing of biographies is a specialist's art, one to which I lay no claim. One might also add that to attempt such a task against the background of adjusting oneself to a new and responsible position does not make the task any easier!

Be this as it may, I feel strongly that some tribute, however unworthy, to a truly great man of God is called for, and that such a tribute should be paid while Dr. Kevan's memory is still fresh in the minds of those who knew and loved him.

Such qualifications as I may have for this task are on the more personal level. To have enjoyed the friendship of Ernest Kevan throughout the twenty and more years when his life was so closely bound up with the London Bible College was an enriching experience. To have witnessed his masterly direction of a college which began with a mere handful of students, and yet within his own lifetime grew to have a complement of over two hundred, was an education in itself. Ernest Kevan was an outstandingly gifted college principal, and his success in that direction is all the more remarkable when one considers that he himself had no formal academic training. As I have tried to show in the following pages, part of his genius lay in his careful choosing of the right men as his colleagues. Another factor which cannot be exaggerated is that behind him, serving his interests devotedly, was a dedicated wife.

Although the name of Ernest Kevan will no doubt be remembered primarily as being that of a college principal, first and foremost he was a pastor. He was never more successful as a pastor than when he occupied the Principal's chair.

One has known of college principals whose experience in the actual work of the ministry was almost entirely theoretical. Not so with Ernest Kevan. He may have had no college training, but he had learned what it was to be a faithful shepherd of the flock.

In each of the three churches which he served he will be remembered supremely for the loving pastoral care he gave to his people. Little wonder that when he came to the College his lectures on Pastoral Theology were probably the most appreciated of all—they sprang out of rich personal experience.

To some it may seem remarkable that the leader of a large interdenominational college should have been recruited from the ranks of the Strict Baptists. Ernest Kevan never failed to acknowledge his indebtedness to his denomination, although he was always ready to co-operate fully with evangelical Christians in other denominations, as of course many other Strict Baptists have done. The whole Christian Church, and evangelicals in particular, must surely recognise their debt to the Strict Baptists who, under God, gave to the London Bible College such a man as Ernest Kevan.

Finally, let me acknowledge the kindness of the many who have helped to make this brief account of Dr. Kevan's life and work possible. First and foremost among them I should mention Mrs. Kevan, whose friendship and willing co-operation is so much appreciated. Thanks are due also to colleagues on the tutorial staff and the old students of the College, as well as to those who knew Ernest Kevan in the various churches he served so faithfully. Last, but by no means least, a word of gratitude is due to Miss Joyce Williamson, Dr. Kevan's secretary and mine, for the painstaking way in which she has prepared the manuscript. Some of the incidents relating to Ernest Kevan's childhood days are culled, by kind permission, from the book of children's addresses published under the title, *Let's Talk*. I am grateful to have received such permission.

The object in publishing this book is not to glorify a man, although one might well be tempted to do that in view of the spiritual stature of the man concerned. But, as one of the speakers at the Memorial Service reminded us, what he was, Dr. Kevan was 'by the grace of God'. One can almost hear him saying: "Do not speak so much of Dr. Kevan, but of Dr. Kevan's Saviour." One thing is certain—that in many parts of this world there will be those who will all their lives 'thank God upon every remembrance' of him.

London
1968

GILBERT W. KIRBY

CONTENTS

CHAPTER ONE

EARLY ENVIRONMENT

Ernest Frederick Kevan was born on January 11th 1903, into what was in many respects a typically middle-class home. The Kevans were a devoted Christian family, enjoying a happy home life. Family prayers were held every day, while on Sunday evenings it was customary for the family to gather around the piano for the singing of 'psalms and hymns and spiritual songs'. As a boy, Ernest had a very good soprano voice; his party piece was, 'O pilot, 'tis a fearful night'. Mr. Kevan, who by profession was general manager to a large chemical manufacturing company, was a deacon at the Strict Baptist Chapel in Chatham Road, Wandsworth Common, in south-west London, and a very active Christian worker. He was leader of the senior Bible class, although his chief piece of Christian work was the editing of a monthly magazine entitled *Seed Thoughts*, a manual for Sunday school teachers. Mrs. Kevan, a lady of strong character, was a Sunday school teacher and conducted women's meetings. She was, in fact, in great demand as a speaker, addressing meetings in many different parts of London. Ernest Kevan's paternal grandfather was Pastor Samuel Kevan, a highly esteemed pastor among the Strict Baptists.

Mr. and Mrs. Kevan brought up their family of three children quite strictly. Ernest's sisters always felt that he, being a boy, probably got off a little more lightly than they did! The children loved to play together, although, like all children, they had their moments! Generally speaking, Ernest was a well-behaved boy, but at times he could be mischievous. One of his earliest recollections was of being in hospital with scarlet-fever. He says, "I was getting better, and the nurse had taken us out for a walk in the afternoon. Because I had made myself dirty by playing with some soot, I had to go without any jam for tea!"

The Kevan children had their full share of fun. They lived in a fairly large house, and one room at the top of the house was set apart as a play-room. There Ernest and his two sisters Ethel and Hilda—one older and the other younger than himself—were allowed to make as much noise as they liked. They played many of the games which children still delight to play—'Dressing up' was always particularly popular, and so was 'Mothers and fathers'. Ernest says, "As I was the only boy I had to be father, and my older sister was mother"; and, he adds, "I rather think the game was not very popular with our young sister." On Sunday evenings before the children were old enough to go to chapel with their parents one of their favourite occupations was playing 'Churches and chapels'. Let Ernest Kevan himself describe a typical Sunday evening:

'We would all three push the chairs into rows like pews. Then we would collect all the hassocks we could find and set everything ready. I remember that the pulpit was an arm-chair which we placed back to the people, and the preacher stood on the seat of it. I am afraid a lot of arguing used to go on as to who was to do this or that. You see, there were not enough of us to go round. I, of course, being the only "man", claimed the right to be the "preacher". One of my sisters played the "organ", and the other was to show the people in and take the collection. But this is where the trouble began. There was nobody to show in, unless we could persuade the lady who looked after us to play with us, and sometimes, dear soul, she did. I used to give out the hymn, and then I had a grand time preaching the "sermon", waving my arms about and thumping the "pulpit" in all the appropriate places. My sisters and I never quarrelled about who should have the money from the collection, for there was never any money in it!'

Because their parents were frequently engaged in outside Christian work, the Kevan children sometimes found themselves alone in the evenings in the care of a lady who delighted to 'mind' them. Mrs. Back was a kindly soul, and when she put the three children to bed invariably she would say, "Now my dears, go to sleep quickly, and I will tell your mother you have been good." One gathers this was not always strictly true, for on occasions the children could be far from good. Yet even on their naughtiest evenings she would still use the same kind words.

Each member of the Kevan family was assigned a special task in the home. It was Ernest's job to wash up; his elder sister Ethel did the drying, while the younger sister Hilda had the task of putting the crockery away. Another of his tasks was cleaning the shoes, a job which always had to be done on Saturday night. There was the minimum of work on Sunday in the Kevan home, for the family was brought up strictly to observe 'the Sabbath'. Typical of the orderly nature of the household was the procedure adopted by Mother and Father for summoning their children into their presence. One ring of the bell meant that the elder daughter was required, two indicated that Ernest's presence was requested, whereas three was the signal for Hilda, his younger sister. As soon as the bell sounded, the children would stop their play, waiting with bated breath to count how many rings there would be! Although he was strict in the way he brought up his family, Mr. Kevan was adored by his children. Ernest probably saw more of his father than did either of his sisters. Somewhat to their envy he would often have long sessions in his father's study. It is significant that when towards the end of his life Dr. Kevan published his book, *The Grace of Law*, he dedicated it to his father who, he pointed out, 'taught him so much theology'.

Ernest was the instigator of most of the games which he and his sisters so much enjoyed in their play-room at the top of the house. At quite a tender age he arranged a show of conjuring at Christmas time to entertain the rest of the family, and from time to time he and his sisters would put on 'plays' from an improvised stage made up principally of orange boxes. As he grew older he took great delight in making things and would spend a good deal of time at carpentry. On one occasion he made a bridge for his model railway. Having completed the task he felt he had to stand on it to prove that it was sufficiently strong! Chemistry was another of his interests. Often he would carry out experiments in an improvised laboratory at home. He was not too popular when, shaking up some acid in a test tube, his thumb slipped and the contents of the test tube spilled down the front of his sister's new dress. He would also frequently play with the boy in the house next door, and he had a number of school friends with whom he enjoyed many different pranks. He was quite adept, incidentally, in the use of a catapult.

Ernest's schooling had begun at what was then known as an elementary school quite near to his home. From there he graduated to Battersea Grammar School. One of the boys at Battersea Grammar School of whom he stood somewhat in awe was Gordon Welch. When Ernest went to the school Gordon was a prefect. Later in life Welch went overseas as a missionary to China with the China Inland Mission, and he and Ernest Kevan became firm friends. Gordon Welch pre-deceased Ernest Kevan by a comparatively few months, and his life-long friend conducted the funeral service. At the age of thirteen Ernest Kevan was transferred to Dulwich College. He was always particularly proud of his old school, which he described as 'the finest school in England'. When he was not wearing a clerical collar Dr. Kevan in later life frequently wore his 'old school tie'. He always referred to the school with great affection. He records how proud he was when he wore for the first time his new school cap with the red and white badge and the blue stripes. He, together with forty other new boys, was tested to see whether he would make the grade for the school choir, but his voice at that time was at the cracked stage, and so he was soon dismissed. This was no great sorrow to him, however, for as he said at the time it seemed much better to go out and play rugger rather than to stay late at school for choir practices.

Ernest Kevan was far from being a 'goody-goody' at school. He recalls that on more than one occasion he had to write, 'I must not talk in school', a hundred times, and he remembers what it felt like to be 'kept in' in order to do an 'extra lesson' for two hours on the school half-holiday. Many years later in the course of a talk to children Ernest Kevan said, "Even now I can almost catch the sound of the friendly crack of the cricket bat as I used to hear it come through the windows of the 'extra lesson' room." In his teens, Ernest Kevan was often taken to be much older. At about the age of fourteen, when the first World War was at its height, he was accosted by some elderly ladies on Wandsworth Common who asked him sharply, "Why aren't you at the front?" His school reports at Dulwich were usually very good, but he was by no means a mere bookworm. He thoroughly enjoyed playing rugger, and on one occasion an over-enthusiastic tackle led to a broken wrist. He sometimes practised 'tackling' at home on his sisters! Ernest also played cricket well and was a good swimmer.

Ernest Kevan left Dulwich College at the age of seventeen— earlier than had been intended, largely because of a serious breakdown in his father's health. Although he had held a good position in business, Mr. Kevan had to retire prematurely because of heart trouble, and this affected the family income. On leaving school Ernest took up an appointment with the Home and Colonial Stores in their tea-tasting department in Mincing Lane in the City of London. He commenced work there on August 26th 1920, and remained with the same firm until September 30th 1927, when he resigned in order to devote himself fully to the work of the Christian ministry. In his diary he proudly recorded the fact that it was on August 30th 1920 that he came home with his first pay-packet!

CHAPTER TWO

CALLED TO THE MINISTRY

As a boy Ernest Kevan was always greatly concerned lest, because of his Christian upbringing, he should pass off as a Christian without in fact having come to a personal knowledge of Jesus Christ as Saviour and Lord. Often he would pray, "O God, please make me a *real* Christian." When about twelve years old he was greatly impressed by a sermon given by the Rev. H. Tydeman Chilvers, who was later to become Pastor of Spurgeon's Tabernacle in London. Shortly afterwards, entirely on his own account, he paid a visit to a somewhat elderly lady in the local chapel who was a close friend of his parents. He confided to her, "If only I could *feel* saved I should believe that I was." This good Christian friend soon put his mind at rest. She told him, "You have got it the wrong way round; we have 'joy and peace in believing'; you believe and then you will know." Later in life he often referred to that conversation which meant a great deal to him.

It was at the age of fourteen that Ernest Kevan was brought to real faith and assurance, largely as the result of listening to a sermon preached by Pastor W. Chisnall, who was then secretary of the Strict Baptist Mission. Shortly after his conversion, on February 25th 1917 he was baptised, and a fortnight later received as a church member, having given his testimony at a church meeting. That same summer, when his parents were staying at Worthing, he took part in a beach service. A rather delightful story is told about him, when he was a lad of fifteen. He was acting as a sidesman one Sunday evening at his local church. A small and rather grubby child, a member of his Sunday school class, was sitting with him in the back row. The Scripture reading at that particular service concerned one of the Lord's miracles of healing. The so-called 'long' prayer which followed seemed rather longer than usual. During the course of it the little boy whispered to Ernest Kevan, "My little brother has got a bad ear; can Jesus make him better?" Immediately he received the reply, "Yes, let us ask Him now." At the time the minister was still praying in the pulpit, but from the back row of the chapel a whispered prayer was being offered on behalf of a little boy's bad ear!

According to his diary, Ernest Kevan preached his first sermon on Wednesday evening, February 15th 1922, in Chatham Road Strict Baptist Chapel, Wandsworth Common, where he had been brought up. Shortly afterwards he ministered at the Strict Baptist Chapel at Horsham, when his text was Job 26.14. Some who were present on that occasion recalled years later the sum and substance of the address. On April 16th 1922, he conducted his first Sunday service at the Strict Baptist Chapel in Bond Street, Brighton. A few weeks later he preached in Bermondsey, taking as his text the words, "Behold your God." As a young man Ernest Kevan identified himself closely with the Strict Baptist Open Air Mission, and he would spend a great deal of his spare time speaking in the open air in various parts of London, usually on Saturdays.

In later life Ernest Kevan often used to refer to three verses of Scripture which were a particular help to him in his youth. St. John, chapter 6, verse 37, he said, helped him to see that his experience rested on the sure promises of God and not on passing feelings. He would frequently speak of his first attendances at the chapel prayer meeting where 'the prayers of the saints were often very long and the seats seemed very hard', but he knew he should be there for thereby he developed a genuine 'love of the brethren' (I John 3.14). Some words in the prophecy of Jeremiah (chapter 33, verse 3) were a special blessing to him at the time when he first became conscious of his call to the ministry.

After several years of itinerant preaching Ernest Kevan entered upon his first pastorate in Walthamstow on the east side of London in June 1924. He moved there on September 3rd 1924, and the Recognition Services were held on October 7th. Church Hill Baptist Church, Walthamstow, claims to be London's oldest Baptist Church. It was an offshoot from an Independent Chapel formed in 1616. At the time of its formation in 1633 at least seven of its eighteen members were in prison for their faith. However, it seems that they gained favour in the eyes of those in charge of them and were permitted various concessions, including 'breaking bread' on the Lord's Day.

The first home of this Baptist cause had been in Wapping, on the banks of the Thames, just outside the city boundary, a district 'chiefly inhabited by seafaring men'. For at least two hundred years the congregation was almost entirely drawn from this area. In the course of time a new 'Meeting House' was erected about a mile away in Little Prescot Street, Goodman's Fields. At that time it enjoyed considerable prosperity, and many well-known Christian men and women were associated with it.

Later, in 1855, a most pretentious sanctuary, seating 1,200 people, was built in Commercial Street, Whitechapel. The pastorate of Pastor Charles Stovel in that church extended altogether for over 51 years. Although he drew large congregations at one stage of his ministry, for some time before his death in 1883 there was a sad decline, and furthermore the district itself was changing in character.

After considerable discussion, the fellowship eventually decided to move to Walthamstow where a site was purchased at Church Hill. On January 15th 1914, the new chapel and school were opened. Shortly afterwards forty members of another local Strict Baptist Church, known as 'Zion', in Maynard Road, Walthamstow, which was in process of dissolution, were welcomed into the membership of the new church. The first pastor at Church Hill had been a Mr. H. D. Tooke who commenced his ministry there in January 1915, resigning in August 1918. The following year Mr. Ernest Wightman became pastor, and he continued in office until April 1922. Two years later Ernest Kevan commenced his work at the church. At that time the church was at a low ebb, with sadly depleted congregations. For just over three years Mr. Kevan stayed on in business, usually getting up at 5 a.m. in order to do two hours' study before breakfast. The strain, however, began to tell on him, and he became the victim of nervous exhaustion. He felt increasingly he had no alternative but to resign his business appointment and give his whole attention to the church. Such a step involved considerable financial sacrifice. God, however, honoured his faith, and his ministry at Walthamstow became more and more fruitful.

Two years after he came to the church, Ernest Kevan had expressed to Jane Basham, one of his congregation, his feelings of affection towards her. None of the church members had the least suspicion of this budding romance for, as always, the pastor had been the soul of discretion. Originally Jane, or 'Jennie' as she was generally know, had been a member of the fellowship meeting at Zion Chapel prior to its amalgamation with Church Hill. Her parents were humble but stalwart Christians. Jennie's mother had died when she was only a few days old. Her father, a Suffolk man, remarried, but his second wife died when Jennie was six. For some years after that an aunt, Miss Holly, brought up the family. Jane Basham was a most active worker at Church Hill— she taught in the Sunday school, helped to run a missionary working party, and for a time led the Young Women's Bible Class. Ernest and Jennie became engaged in January 1926 when Ernest was twenty-three, and they married on May 21st 1927, the ceremony being conducted by Pastor W. S. Baker, a well-known pastor among the Strict Baptists at that time.

While at Church Hill, Ernest Kevan wrote a history of the church entitled, *London's Oldest Baptist Church*. During the course of his ministry—on September 7th 1929—a branch chapel was opened free of debt three miles away in Kings Road, Chingford. During the years in which Mr. Keven laboured at Walthamstow the church's membership steadily increased, and a full and varied programme of weekly activities was carried through.

The 300th Anniversary of the founding of the church was celebrated in September 1933. Among the special speakers who addressed a series of meetings which were held were the Rev. Dr. W. T. Whitley, then the honorary secretary of the Baptist Historical Society, the Rev. J. Ernest James, a Congregationalist and President of the London Free Church Federation, the Bishop of Barking and the Rev. J. Chalmers Lyon, a Presbyterian. In addition, of course, some of the leading Strict Baptist pastors of the day participated in this series of gatherings, including the Rev. George E. J. Bird, later to become pastor of Bethesda Chapel, Ipswich, and a life-long friend of Ernest Kevan. Ernest Kevan himself delivered a masterly address in which he spoke in glowing terms of those Puritan forebears who had originally come together to form the church. He argued strongly that Calvinistic doctrines were not incompatible with evangelistic enterprise, and concluded with these significant words :

B

'The times in which we live call upon us for our witness. Let it ring true to modern needs so that men of today may see that we care for them. Times have changed, customs and modes of thought have changed, but the deep spiritual longings of men and the grace of God remain the same. We do not need a new Gospel, but we must surely seek to present that old Gospel in words and pictures suitable to the present time. Obsolete phrases and methods are just as out of place as an Elizabethan costume would be in this congregation tonight. Let us seek to present the timeless Gospel in a way finely adapted to the ever-changing moods of men and women. Our message is the same as our fathers', but our mood of presenting that message, and our methods of evangelistic effort, must be those of the twentieth century.'

Before leaving the subject of Ernest Kevan's ministry at Church Hill, Walthamstow, reference must be made to an outstanding piece of work which he carried out among the men of the district. In the Autumn of 1932, at a time when there was a great deal of unemployment, he sought the church's agreement for the holding of regular meetings for men for which he would be personally responsible. Assisted by a small band of volunteers, all of whom were equipped with handbills, he contacted men of all walks of life in the parks, recreation grounds, public libraries, as well as in the streets, inviting them to a men's meeting to be held on October 19th 1932. That day fifteen men attended. Mr. Kevan explained why the meeting had been started, and that it would be a quite informal gathering with refreshments beforehand. There would also be bright singing, solos and short talks. As the weeks passed attendances rapidly increased. Eventually Pastor Kevan and his workers were greatly exercised as to how to deal with so great a number of men. There were men of all ages and all types attending. Some had 'no fixed abode' and 'lived rough' yet Ernest Kevan was held in great esteem by all these men. Despite the fact that he was the minister of the church he adapted himself remarkably in getting alongside them. They nicknamed him the 'Sergeant-Major', and he accepted the designation without demur. He and his helpers collected clothing, boots and food parcels for those in greatest need. The weekly meetings were packed almost to suffocation. Often one could see men, considerably advanced in years, completely broken down when something happened in the meeting which reminded them of their younger days. Sometimes one of the men themselves would sing a solo. Mr. Kevan also made a point of visiting them when they were sick. More than once, with jacket off, sleeves rolled up and an apron around his waist, he would get on his hands and knees and scrub a floor. At other times he would change the bedding of a sick man. This sort of thing went on week after week. Little wonder that he was greatly thought of by all.

Ernest Kevan gave to his men's meeting the title, 'The Held-out-Hand'. He explained that it was the hand to welcome and the hand to help which was proffered to men. Each member had a badge which he proudly wore in his lapel. Many of the men idolised Mr. Kevan. Although he never lost his dignity he demonstrated clearly that he had the common touch.

Needless to say, it came as a shock when the church was told that their pastor, after ten years among them which had been so richly blessed, had received and accepted a call to serve the Strict Baptist Chapel at New Cross. It should be added that Mrs. Kevan had also greatly endeared herself to young and old alike throughout her husband's ministry at Walthamstow. Mr. Kevan's parents had also come to live with their son and daughter-in-law at the Manse, and they, too, wholeheartedly identified themselves with the work of the church as far as health would allow. Ernest Kevan concluded his most fruitful ministry at Church Hill Baptist Church at the end of May 1934.

CHAPTER THREE

NEW CROSS DAYS

Ernest Kevan commenced his ministry at Zion Chapel, New Cross, on June 3rd 1934. His pastorate of over nine and a half years included the difficult war years when night after night London was under heavy enemy attack. In the face of seemingly insurmountable difficulties he led the church forward with remarkable success. A former deacon of Zion has described the call to Mr. Kevan as 'the first move towards unity in a very disunited church'. Although a young man he had the strength, grace and tact which the situation demanded, and under his able leadership the church members were encouraged to work together as a team.

Mr. and Mrs. Kevan senior joined their son and daughter-in-law in the Manse at New Cross, but Mr. Kevan died about two years later, and his widow died in February 1940. That same year, when the London area was being bombarded night after night, the Manse was damaged and had to be evacuated, and the Kevans moved into a flat.

Ernest Kevan was no gardener, but largely because he felt the need of some form of exercise he made a valiant effort to develop an interest in gardening. On one occasion the Rev. and Mrs. Oliver Clark, close friends of the Kevans, visited them at their flat. Since Mr. Clark was himself a keen gardener, Ernest Kevan was most anxious to show him his own gardening efforts. The ground behind the block of flats in which the Kevans lived had been parcelled out into a number of plots. Ernest pointed out that he had been busily engaged in hoeing one of these plots. To his intense dismay he learned from his friend Mr. Clark that he had, in fact, hoed up his neighbour's crop of carrots thinking that they were grass! Incidentally, towards the end of his life Ernest Kevan again turned to gardening as a recreation, and he became particularly interested in the cultivation of roses.

It was probably while at New Cross that Mr. Kevan made the greatest contribution to his own denomination—the Strict Baptists. In March 1938 he became President of the Metropolitan Association of Strict Baptist Churches, an office which he fulfilled with great acceptance. His presidential address entitled 'Doctrine and Development' revealed his deep attachment to and concern for his denomination. Together with the Rev. Oliver Clark and the Rev. Percy Crees, he helped in the compilation of a young people's hymn book comprising some six hundred different hymns. Much of the work on this was done in the Manse at Over in Cambridgeshire where Mr. Crees was then pastor.

Like his father before him Ernest Kevan was keenly interested in the Strict Baptist Mission's work in India, and in the Strict Baptist Open Air Mission. He was also instrumental in bringing together the Sunday School Committees of the London, Cambridgeshire and Suffolk Associations to form the Strict Baptist National Sunday School Association. He took the chair at the inaugural meeting of the Fellowship of Youth which was to prove such a blessing to the denomination. In this work he enjoyed the close co-operation of the Rev. George E. J. Bird. Mr. and Mrs. Kevan attended the first House-Party of the Fellowship of Youth at Mundesley on Sea, and they were host and hostess at a subsequent House-Party at Swanage.

In spite of the difficulties of the war years, under Pastor Kevan's vigorous leadership the church at New Cross prospered greatly. Many pay tribute to his exceptional gifts as a preacher and organiser, and to the fact that during his ministry at Zion an increasing number of young people were attracted to the church. Mr. Kevan also excelled as a visitor and was constantly in the homes of his people. In this he had the able assistance of his devoted wife. He maintained a regular contact by correspondence with the evacuated members of the church and congregation, including those serving in the forces at home and overseas. Prior to the war he had started a men's meeting on similar lines to that which had been so successful in Walthamstow. These were the worst years of the depression with its attendant poverty and unemployment. Dozens of men were to be found in Deptford Broadway—near the Chapel—waiting to sign on at the Labour Exchange. In a short time over a hundred such men were regularly attending the meetings of 'The Held-out-Hand' on Thursday afternoons. Parcels of clothing and food vouchers were given to particularly needy cases. Among these men there were definite conversions and some became regular worshippers at the Chapel.

Another feature of Ernest Kevan's pastorate in Deptford was the regular open-air services held on Saturday and Sunday evenings. Often members of the church were kept busy answering questions till late at night.

Probably one of the greatest joys of Ernest Kevan's pastorate at New Cross was his work in the beginners' department of the Sunday school where he attracted as many as ninety youngsters between the ages of five and seven. He simply loved these children and was never happier than when he was with them. Later when he went to the London Bible College he often used to say that what he missed most was his regular contact with boys and girls. In 1964, the year before he died, he conducted no less than thirteen Sunday school anniversaries on consecutive Sundays. On one occasion the Scripture Union invited him to address a great rally of children at the Central Hall, Westminster, and the youngsters were so moved by his address that quite spontaneously they applauded him at the conclusion of it. On another occasion, after addressing a children's rally held in connection with the Abinger Convention, he was similarly applauded by the children.

Ernest Kevan introduced to his church at New Cross, Campaigners, an evangelical and interdenominational uniformed youth movement which had been started by the late Prebendary Colin C. Kerr. Soon he had a Campaigner Clan of some fifty youngsters complete with drum and fife band.

During his pastorate at Zion, Ernest Kevan regularly wrote a paragraph for the *Kentish Mercury*, entitled 'Hear What Comfortable Words'—using the pen-name Kerux. These simple messages found general acceptance among the readers of the paper and were much appreciated.

In spite of the heavy demands of pastoral work, Ernest Kevan found time to study while at New Cross, first for his Bachelor of Divinity degree, and later for his Master of Theology. He had had no formal college education, but by dint of disciplined study he succeeded in obtaining his B.D. at the first attempt in 1935. Seven years later he submitted his thesis for his M.Th., which was accepted.

Although a Strict Baptist by conviction, and uncompromising as far as his evangelicalism was concerned, Ernest Kevan played an active part in interdenominational work while at Zion Chapel. He served at one time as Chairman of the Deptford Council of Christian Churches, and he was twice Chairman of the Deptford Ministers' Fraternal. He also served as Chairman of Lucas Vale L.C.C. (as it then was) School Care Committee, and for nearly two years was a member of the Deptford Youth Committee.

The last Sunday of the year, December 26th 1943, marked the end of Ernest Kevan's pastorate at New Cross. The church was distressed at the thought of parting with a greatly beloved pastor, yet there was the realisation that Mr. and Mrs. Kevan were being led by God to 'pastures new'. A large company assembled to bid farewell to the Pastor and his wife, and many warm tributes were paid to them. Another illustrious chapter had closed, but an even greater one was shortly to open.

One who was a humble member of his church at New Cross pays this tribute to his former pastor: 'Many knew him as an outstanding leader, teacher and scholar, but I am sure there are a number like myself who remember him as a truly Christian man, proving himself to be a wise, sympathetic and understanding brother in the Lord, backed by a truly Christian woman.'

CHAPTER FOUR

AT TRINITY ROAD

Early in 1943 the church secretary at Trinity Road Chapel, Upper Tooting, had invited the Rev. R. J. Park to preach 'with a view' to becoming Minister. Mr. Park replied, saying that he had just accepted a call to Muswell Hill Baptist Church, but he enclosed the names of four men whom he had recommended for consideration by his deacons as possible successors to himself at Forest Hill.

As it happened, three of these had already preached at Trinity Road, but the fourth, Ernest Kevan, was unknown to the deacons there, apart from the fact that he was a Strict Baptist. The Church Secretary, Mr. A. H. Long, having conferred with his co-deacon Mr. Ashley Baker, and also with the Rev. Ernest Rose, both of whom knew Mr. Kevan, and having received strong recommendations in his favour, requested the deacons to allow him to attend and report upon a meeting which he knew Mr. Kevan was about to address at Mitcham Lane Baptist Church.

Mr. Kevan's subject on that occasion was 'The Faith'. The report Mr. Long gave was so favourable that his fellow-deacons unanimously instructed him to seek an interview with Ernest Kevan at his home in New Cross. This he did without delay, telling him plainly how the Lord appeared to be moving in the hearts and minds of the deacons at Trinity Road Chapel. Mr. Kevan showed little interest but agreed to preach at Trinity Road six months later (September 1943). Meanwhile the conviction that Ernest Kevan was God's man for the church grew so strong that a letter was circulated to every member of Trinity Road Chapel, urging attendance on the day of his visit and at a special church meeting to follow four days later. The result was that the church members unanimously invited Ernest Kevan to become their minister.

As with the call to Walthamstow, so it was in the case of 'Trinity Road'—the invitation had come entirely unsought. In accepting it, Mr. Kevan realised that the pastorate there might not be a lengthy one. He was conscious of a growing 'pull' in the direction of academic work. His links with the London Bible College then in process of formation were becoming increasingly strong. The Directors of the College at their meeting on January 13th 1944 invited him to join the teaching faculty which he subsequently agreed to do. At that time the College was merely producing a number of correspondence courses and arranging series of evening lectures. The Directors at their February meeting warmly received Ernest Kevan's memorandum—'Directions to Students'—and expressed appreciation of his wise handling of the correspondence courses. In the autumn of 1944, but a few months after settling at Trinity Road Chapel, he received and accepted an invitation from the Directors of the College to become a part-time tutor.

The question might be asked as to the effect his going to a non-Strict Baptist Chapel had on his relationships with the denomination of his upbringing. As one of his colleagues remarked, "It caused nothing more than a flutter." There were those among the Strict Baptists who had cherished the hope that he might stay with them and become a tutor in their Bible Institute, but there was no bitterness expressed when he left their ranks and went to the Chapel in Trinity Road, Upper Tooting. It would be true to say that to the end he remained *persona grata* in Strict Baptist circles. Indeed, many would claim that at heart he never forsook his Strict Baptist position. Certainly when he became Principal of the London Bible College he received numerous students from Strict Baptist chapels who were later to undertake pastorates in his old denomination. He did however remark on one occasion to a close friend that he felt at times that he was 'nobody's child'. His name, of course, appeared on the ministerial list of the Baptist Union, but he never took any active part in the affairs of the Union, nor did he ever serve as minister of a church which was in affiliation with it.

When Ernest Kevan came to Trinity Road the war was still in progress. While he and his wife were on their holiday in July 1944, their house was damaged by blast from a flying bomb. A score or more members of the church worked in relays, clearing up the debris and fixing waterproof sheeting to the window frames.

In spite of all the difficulties the church prospered remarkably during the pastorate, and Mr. and Mrs. Kevan endeared themselves to all. In two years thirty-nine new members were welcomed.

A weekly Bible School held on Sunday mornings was enthusiastically attended by people of all ages. New vitality, after the strain of war years, was imparted to all branches of the church's life. Besides the spiritual nourishment provided through the pulpit ministry, valuable instruction was given in various series of articles in the church magazine. Door to door visitation was undertaken, and a literature stall was provided at the church. When, for the first time in the history of the district, permission was given for a fair to be held on Wandsworth Common, Mr. Kevan promptly interviewed the manager and obtained his consent to a service being held for the caravan dwellers. The Chapel choir sang, and the minister gave a simple talk and warm-hearted invitation to turn to the Lord and to attend the services at Trinity Road.

Ernest Kevan's talks to the children at the morning service were masterpieces. At one period he had a miniature letter box standing on the table before the pulpit, into which the children were invited to place their 'letters to the Minister' as well as their answers to the questions he set following his addresses. He prized the letters received, most highly. His children's addresses were models of simplicity and clarity and were of topical interest, combined with wholesome humour and obvious spiritual lessons.

When it was announced that as from January 1946 the London Bible College would receive full-time day students, and that Mr. Kevan had been invited to become Resident Tutor, the news was received by his church with mixed feelings. While reluctantly accepting his resignation from the pastorate, they rejoiced to know that Mr. and Mrs. Kevan intended to continue in membership with them, and they felt it an honour that they should be identified with their minister's wider ministry in the training of candidates for Christian service at home and abroad. Dr. Kevan did, in fact, remain a member of his old church at Trinity Road until the time of his death, and over the years he never ceased to take an active interest in its affairs. Whenever he was free to do so he and Mrs. Kevan would attend the Sunday services and weekly prayer meeting. During the time when the church was without a pastor following the departure of the Rev. W. Price Lewis in 1963, Dr. (as he had then become) Kevan gave a great deal of help to the church, frequently conducting the Sunday services and Bible studies in the week. In fact, on the last Sunday of his earthly life he preached at Trinity Road and had fully expected to preside at the induction of the newly appointed minister, the Rev. Kenneth I. Paterson, the following week.

On the day of his death the deacons met and it was recorded :

'That the deacons of Trinity Road Chapel have learned with great sorrow of the home-call of Dr. Ernest F. Kevan, their fellow-member for twenty-two years, and their one-time beloved Minister.

They wish to record their appreciation, and their thanks to God for the generosity of affection manifested towards their church by Dr. Kevan during many years, and for the wisdom of his counsel readily available and freely given whenever it was sought.

They recall with esteem his distinguished scholarship and his strength of character, joined with a humility of spirit and a gracious personality, which endeared him to all who were privileged to know him.'

Writing subsequently in the monthly magazine of Trinity Road Chapel, Mr. H. Carey Oakley paid tribute to his former minister :

'Dr. Kevan's life and witness was based upon a personal experience of God's saving grace in Jesus Christ, a confidence in God's sovereignty, a fidelity to the Scriptures as God's word and a daily walk with God that made him the humble and gracious man he was. To know him and to work with him was a privilege and an inspiration. His work lives on in the lives of countless men and women whose Christian character he helped to mould.'

Rarely has a pastorate of such brief duration had such a profound and lasting effect upon a church. Perhaps this was all the more remarkable in view of the fact that Ernest Kevan's immediate predecessor, Henry Oakley, had laboured faithfully at Trinity Road for forty-eight years.

CHAPTER FIVE

THE CAPTAIN PICKS HIS TEAM

It is interesting to note that to those who, in the early days, were responsible for planning the London Bible College, the name of Ernest Kevan had come to mind at the outset as a possible lecturer. When in the Autumn of 1944 Mr. Kevan was invited by the Directors of the College to become a part-time tutor, with typical foresight he raised the issue of legitimate differences of opinion among evangelicals on such points as the interpretation of prophecy. He was given the assurance that there would be 'liberty to state opposite views side by side, and, if the course of the argument or a student's question demanded it, the tutor would be free to state his own view without fear or favour'. From the earliest days, Ernest Kevan had the vision that the College should train not only future pastors and missionaries, but also those who would be equipped to go into the schools of the country as specialists in teaching Religious Knowledge. He was quick to see the need for forming a Teaching Faculty. In those early days, among his advisers he had the Rev. George R. Beasley-Murray, later to become Principal of Spurgeon's College, the Rev. Canon Frank Colquhoun, now Chancellor of Southwark Cathedral, the late Rev. L. F. E. Wilkinson, who became Principal of Oak Hill College, and myself, the present Principal of the College.

It became known in June 1945 that the China Inland Mission at Newington Green were willing to place at the disposal of the College, for a temporary period and at a nominal rental, premises in Highbury New Park in North London. Here was a house of four storeys, a sub-basement and rooms suitable for use as classrooms as well as for bedroom accommodation. The Rev. William Oram, now minister of Mitcham Lane Baptist Church, Streatham, describes what it was like to be one of the first students at the College.

'With some five or six other men I was privileged to be among the first intake of resident students at the London Bible College, when first opened in premises belonging to the China Inland Mission at Highbury New Park on 21st January, 1946. In those first two terms we were joined by a few other students from the National Young Life Campaign at Kew, for daily lectures. Mr. Kevan himself conducted most of the studies, though one or two additional lecturers also came in for certain subjects. The smallness of the College in no sense detracted from its high aims academically, morally or spiritually ... In those early days there was a sense of domestic family life.'

Another of those original students, the Rev. Murdo R. Gordon, now Principal of the Bible Institute of South Africa, describes his first contacts with the College Principal :

'My first meeting with Mr. Kevan took place in 1945 when I was interviewed about my application to enter the London Bible College. About that meeting I remember very little. The second meeting was much more memorable. A few days before the time came to join the College, then at Highbury New Park, I called round to leave some possessions in my room. The door was opened by no less a person than the Principal, but how unlike the carefully groomed person we usually knew, he appeared on this occasion! He had obviously been white-washing a room!'

Ernest Kevan did not keep a full diary throughout his life, but in the early days of the College he did jot down some most illuminating thoughts which reveal his hopes as well as his fears at that time :

'Friday, 26th April 1946—Up at 6.30 a.m. Prayer 7–7.30 a.m. Gal. 3.27—I have "put on Christ" and therefore He should be seen when I am seen. God reminded me again that the College work is His, and I have but to do His bidding. O God, keep me in this trustful place.

Monday, 29th April 1946—Up at 6.0 a.m. Prayer 7–7.30 a.m. It was hard to pray. Summer Term begins.

Tuesday, 30th April 1946—Up at 5.30 a.m. Prayer 6–6.30 a.m. I told the Lord I trusted Him for grace and strength and wisdom. I told the Lord I trusted Him with the lectures as I now put myself into the work . . . Lord, make me one who is wholly devoted to Thee.

Wednesday, 1st May 1946—Up at 5.30 a.m. Prayer 6–6.30 a.m. Read in II Kings, chapter 9, of the unexpected divine call to Jehu. Wondered what the message was for me. O Lord, keep me humble, but ready enough to do Thy will wherever it takes me. Lord, make me just a CHANNEL. Help me to lead my students closer to Thee; give me Thy grace as I preside at the meals. O give my mind Thy light for the lectures, and power of clear expression.'

It is clear that Ernest Kevan was deeply conscious of his need of divine guidance for each step of the way in these formative weeks and months of the College's life.

Shortly after taking over the premises in Highbury New Park, the College received a generous offer from Mr. (later Sir) John W. Laing, who from the outset had shown a keen interest in the development of the College. He offered premises at 19 Marylebone Road, London, close to Baker Street Station, for a period of three to five years, rent-free. Needless to say, the Directors agreed to accept this munificent offer. This, in turn, led to the appointment of Ernest Kevan as Resident Tutor as from January 1st 1946. A few months later—at a meeting of the Directors held at St. Andrew's Rectory, Holborn—the Chairman, the Rev. J. Russell Howden, proposed that Ernest Kevan should be appointed College Principal rather than Resident Tutor. The Board unanimously approved this proposal. In the autumn of 1946 the premises in Marylebone Road, having been redecorated, were made available for temporary use by the College. The newly-appointed Principal put forward the proposal that the College should appoint two part-time Assistant Tutors, one to lecture on the Old Testament and related subjects, and the other to concentrate more especially on New Testament subjects. In due course Mr. H. L. Ellison, B.A., B.D., was appointed as part-time Old Testament lecturer, and shortly afterwards the Rev. E. W. Hadwen, B.D., joined the full-time staff as Senior Tutor. In spite of having strong denominational ties himself, Ernest Kevan from the outset was determined to maintain the truly interdenominational nature of the College. Mr. Ellison had formerly been a Church of England clergyman but was now associated with the

Christian Brethren, while the Rev. E. W. Hadwen was a Canon in the Church of England. The next appointment to be made was that of Mr. P. G. Eyers, a schoolmaster who worshipped with the Christian Brethren and whose early death five years later was a great loss to the College. At a very early stage Ernest Kevan drew up a recommendation which was approved by the Directors regarding the denominational affiliation of the students who entered the College. It read as follows: 'In order to prevent the interdenominational position of the College being compromised in any way, students shall be advised verbally when entering the College that it is undesirable that any change in their denominational affiliation shall be made during their period of training.'

In these early years the Principal, in addition to his lecturing responsibilities, gave a great deal of his time to consider the future policy of the College and in grappling with the problems of accommodation, since the student body was growing at a phenomenal rate. One of the students at this time, later to be appointed the College's first Resident Warden, Mr. Raymond Ash, recalls memories of life in the original premises at 19 Marylebone Road:

'My student days were in the early years of the College, when, although there were many things it did not have, it did have a front garden! The rain not infrequently came through the ceiling, and the pipes on the walls of the old basement used to wander about going nowhere in particular! Mr. and Mrs. Kevan lived in the College in those days, and I remember how I missed him when he was not around. We did not really know just how much he and his wife concerned themselves with our welfare. With typical student effrontery we called him "Uncle Ernie", which in some curious way represented our regard for him. As years went by, successive generations of students experienced his unfailing thought for them.'

One of the outstanding gifts which the College's first Principal had was the ability to choose the right men for his 'team'. He was led to approach men of widely differing backgrounds, all of whom were to prove themselves over the years. One of his early choices was that of the Rev. J. H. Stringer, M.A., B.D., a Methodist minister who had been serving in Middlesbrough. Shortly after that he approached the Rev. H. Dermot McDonald, B.A., who was then minister of the Baptist Tabernacle at Woolwich but was known to be interested in the possibility of lecturing at a theological college. Within a comparatively short while following his appointment Mr. McDonald, in spite of a very full programme of lectures, studied for and gained a B.D. Honours degree. In 1954 he was appointed Vice-Principal, and three years later was awarded by the University the degree of Doctor of Philosophy. In 1967 a still greater honour was bestowed upon him in that he was awarded the degree of Doctor of Divinity by the University of London.

The Principal succeeded in gathering together not only a team of men who were truly evangelical and representative of different denominational backgrounds, but such as would in coming years add yet further to their academic laurels, and in so doing enhance the academic reputation of the College. Mr. Kevan had always envisaged that in due time at least some members of the Faculty would be drawn from the ranks of former students of the College. His dream began to be fulfilled when Mr. Donald Guthrie, on the completion of his B.D. course in 1949, remained at the College to take his place on the teaching staff. Mr. Guthrie was awarded his M.Th. in 1951 and ten years later gained his Doctorate of Philosophy.

When Mr. Hadwen's health compelled him to resign from teaching at the College, Mr. Kevan approached another ordained member of the Church of England to join the staff, the Rev. Owen J. Thomas, B.A., now College Chaplain. He became a tutor in 1951 and in those days was largely responsible for teaching French and other subjects for the London B.A. degree which was then taken by a number of students.

In the summer of 1952 the Principal introduced two new features into the life of the College. He himself gave the first of what was to be a series of Annual College Lectures, taking as his theme, 'The Doctrine of the Holy Spirit in Relation to our Preaching'. He also arranged the first College Quiet Day, which was led by the late Rev. L. F. E. Wilkinson. Now a terminal Quiet Day is a much appreciated feature of College life.

When failing health compelled the Rev. J. H. Stringer to resign, the Rev. J. Clement Connell, M.A., who was at the time minister of Herne Hill Baptist Church, London, was invited by the Principal to become a member of the tutorial staff. In 1954 Mr.

C

Kevan asked him to become Director of Studies, an office which he has held with distinction over the years. That same year Mr. Harold H. Rowdon, B.A., who had been teaching in a grammar school and was linked with the Christian Brethren, was invited to join the tutorial staff, with responsibility for lecturing mainly in Church History and Christian Ethics. Mr. Rowdon obtained his Ph.D. degree in 1965. He has served the College for many years as Resident Warden. The appointment of the Rev. John C. J. Waite, B.D., in 1955 as Old Testament lecturer brought another old student on to the staff. When after a period of faithful service at the College Mr. Waite left, it was in order to become Principal of the South Wales Bible College.

The mid-fifties saw a number of changes, both in the tutorial as well as in the domestic and administrative staff of the College. The first lady tutor was appointed—Miss Rosina Parker, M.A. Miss Parker, an Honours graduate in English, was largely responsible for the Arts courses which the College was at that time providing. When some years later the College decided to concentrate upon preparing men and women for theological degrees and diplomas, Miss Parker returned to the teaching profession. She was quickly replaced by yet another old student in the person of Miss Margaret E. Manton, B.A., B.D., who, in turn, served for five years, concentrating on teaching Greek and also on the evening class lectures in preparation for the Certificate of Proficiency in Religious Knowledge, as well as serving as Resident Warden for women students. Miss Manton is now Vice-Principal of Ridgelands Bible College.

Mention should also be made of another lady whom the Principal invited to serve the College—Mrs. Dannatt, F.L.C.M., L.R.A.M. Ernest Kevan had known her since before her marriage. She had been associated with him in the formation of the Fellowship of Youth Movement in the Strict Baptist denomination. Early in the history of the College he had approached her with a view to her giving some help in voice production but at that time her children were too young for her to accept even a part-time teaching appointment. However, some years later Mrs. Dannatt gladly acceded to a further request from the Principal, and for ten years she served most acceptably as a part-time member of the Tutorial Staff with special responsibility for speech training.

Another appointment made on the recommendation of Dr. Kevan was that of the Rev. R. P. Martin, then serving as the minister of Dunstable Baptist Church. Mr. Martin came primarily as lecturer in Dogmatic Theology. While on the tutorial staff he, too, gained his Doctorate of Philosophy. Mr. L. C. Allen, a Cambridge honours graduate, and associated with the Christian Brethren, joined the tutorial staff in 1960 and was given special responsibility for teaching Greek and Hebrew.

The Principal when he served as minister of Trinity Road Chapel gained a high regard and affection for the son of his distinguished predecessor—Mr. H. Carey Oakley, M.A. Mr. Oakley at that time was Senior Classics master at the City of London school, but was persuaded by Ernest Kevan to give some part-time assistance to the College in teaching Greek. There was a close bond between the two men. Mr. Oakley, although now retired, retains links with the College through continuing to be invited to attend meetings of the Faculty.

Ernest Kevan was always anxious that the College should maintain a strong missionary interest, and to that end he invited the Rev. John Savage in 1955 to provide a regular course of missionary lectures, later calling upon him to become Director of Missionary Studies.

There have been those who from time to time have suggested that Mr. Kevan lacked enthusiasm for evangelistic activities, but facts disprove any such contention. The Principal from the very beginning encouraged the students to undertake evangelistic treks and missions in their Easter and summer vacations. In 1957 he invited Mr. Timothy J. Buckley, who had for several years been on the staff as Extension Secretary, to become in addition Supervisor of Evangelism.

Ernest Kevan not only had a flair for choosing the right people for his team, but also for retaining their love and loyalty. This was not only true of the tutorial staff. His personal secretary, Miss Joyce Williamson, for example, came to the College in 1947 and served the Principal as his Private Secretary devotedly up till the time of his death. She and her family were and are active members of Mr. Kevan's old church at Trinity Road.

In the early days of the College there were several changes in the Secretariat. It was a particularly happy day for the Principal when Mr. Donald Baker agreed to leave his post at The Crusaders'

Union and become College Secretary. The two men worked together in the closest possible harmony over the years.

It is significant that the last appointments to the tutorial staff made on the Principal's recommendation were of men drawn from the ranks of old students. The Rev. Arthur E. Cundall, B.A., B.D., now Old Testament lecturer, was a student from 1960–1961, and the Rev. Geoffrey W. Grogan, B.D., M.Th., now lecturer in Dogmatics, was at the College from 1949–1951. To complete the picture, it should be recorded that Mr. David Jackson, M.A. who was a 'House Chairman' in Dr. Kevan's day, has since joined the Faculty as a Lecturer, bringing the total of former students now serving as tutors to four.

Ernest Kevan did not confine his interest and attention to the full-time courses at the College. He always showed a deep personal concern both for the evening classes and for the correspondence courses. When he saw the need for someone to give more time and attention to this side of the work it was to an old student that he turned for help. Mr. John Potter, one of the first students in the Highbury days, came back to his old College in 1965 to serve as Registrar, after having served for several years in the pastoral ministry.

Ernest Kevan was personally interested in every aspect of the work. Nothing escaped his notice, and no one failed to evoke his interest and concern. He aimed to make the staff, tutorial, administrative and domestic, feel themselves to be members of one family. Every Monday afternoon he called everyone together to meet in the Chapel for a quarter of an hour for prayer. Invariably he himself would lead these sessions, and would see to it that the special needs of each department were made known to all.

CHAPTER SIX

A GOOD ALL-ROUNDER

From the day when he assumed responsibilities as Principal of the London Bible College, Ernest Kevan knew the direction in which he should go. On the one hand he knew that his task was to build up a college loyal without reservations of any kind to the complete trustworthiness of the Bible, but at the same time he realised that the courses at the College must be conducted at the highest possible level of academic attainment. Throughout the years he never wavered from this objective. His own position as a conservative evangelical was never in question, but neither was his determination to reach the highest levels of scholarship. We had already noted the gift which he had for choosing the right men for the Teaching Faculty. He encouraged his colleagues not only to give of their best in lecturing to the students but also to equip themselves even more adequately for the task by further studies and even greater scholastic attainments. At the same time Dr. Kevan was enabled to achieve a sense of balance in the College. While he was training men and women for University degrees he saw the need to acquaint them with a practical working knowledge of the Bible. Every prospective B.D. student, in addition to his degree course, took and still takes an additional Bible course set by the College.

While Ernest Kevan himself loved the pastoral office, and excelled in it, he always had a great concern to train young men and women for positions in the teaching profession at home and for missionary service overseas. At one stage he cherished the vision of the London Bible College being fully recognised as a teacher training college, but this dream did not find fulfilment. Together with his colleagues, however, he did establish a Department of Advanced Studies with the set purpose of encouraging honours graduates to pursue higher qualifications in theology.

Special advice is given in the preparation of theses and suggestions made as to profitable fields of study. Dr. Kevan was also enthusiastic in encouraging the publication of *Vox Evangelica*, a scholarly theological journal containing biblical and historical essays by members of the Faculty, which aims to make a worthwhile contribution to contemporary religious thinking and to evangelical scholarship.

Almost as soon as the College occupied its new premises at 19 Marylebone Road, it became clear to the Principal and his colleagues that the available accommodation was inadequate. There were two possible alternatives: to reduce the intake of students, or to search for an alternative site in order to build premises adequate for the needs of a growing number of students. As far as the Principal was concerned, he dreamed of a college of at least three hundred residential students. He spent hours considering with the College Secretary, Mr. Donald Baker, possible plans for development. He personally surveyed in detail every plan that was put forward. He investigated a variety of schemes for moving the College to the outskirts of London. Together with Mr. Baker, he travelled miles visiting such places as Ruislip, Stanmore, Croydon, Worcester Park, Uxbridge, Surbiton, Mill Hill and Beckenham. In spite of testing many possibilities, it seemed time and again that the Principal and the Board of Governors were brought back to a reconsideration of the original site. Accordingly, much thought was given to ways and means of making better use of the existing premises and, where possible, extending them. Houses in Nottingham Place were purchased in order to provide additional hostel accommodation. In every step that was contemplated the Principal took a deep personal interest.

Undoubtedly one of the crowning achievements of Ernest Kevan's career came in 1961 when it was announced following detailed inspection that the Minister of Education had decided to recognise the London Bible College as 'an efficient establishment of Further Education'. The inspection of the College had been carried out by four of Her Majesty's Inspectors of the Ministry of Education, and it covered every aspect of the College's curriculum and teaching methods. The L.B.C. was now well and truly on the educational map.

One might gain the impression that, having become Principal of the London Bible College, Ernest Kevan from that time onwards had a 'one track mind'. It is certainly true that he devoted his time and his energies primarily to the interests of the College. At the same time he did have wider interests, although even so these had some bearing on the work of the College. He resisted the temptation to join too many councils and committees which would demand regular attendance on his part, although he allowed his name to be associated with several councils of reference. He did, however, serve on the Executive Councils of the Evangelical Alliance and the Wycliffe Bible Translators. His links with the Wycliffe Bible Translators had repercussions in the College in so far that over the years a number of L.B.C. students have gone overseas with the Society, and there has always been a lively interest in the work among the student body.

In many ways Ernest Kevan was a typical Englishman. Perhaps for that reason he did not take too kindly to the American scene when he visited the United States as far back as 1949. At that time when the College was in its infancy, the Principal toured a number of American cities in order to acquaint American Christians with the work of the rapidly-developing College. He greatly appreciated the generous hospitality which he enjoyed, but he found it difficult to acclimatise himself to certain aspects of the American way of life. His tour took him to many of the major American cities, including New York, Washington, Chicago, Philadelphia and Minneapolis. He addressed students in the various colleges which he visited, and spoke at numerous luncheons and public meetings. He also gave a series of addresses at the well-known Winona Lake Conference Centre.

At the beginning of 1960 Mr. Kevan paid a visit to India. This was an experience which he greatly enjoyed and which he found both enlightening and disturbing. He was deeply moved by the spiritual and material needs of the people. His ministry there was richly blessed. He addressed innumerable meetings and conferences, including the Annual Conference of the Evangelical Fellowship of India. Writing home to Mr. Donald Baker, the College Secretary, shortly before he left India, Ernest Kevan said, 'I am still well and in the midst of a busy series of meetings here. I am to speak ten times, and then in addition on Saturday I shall address 1,300 Indian students—mostly Hindus—at a college graduation ceremony.' On the way home he visited the Holy Land, another experience which he greatly appreciated.

Plans had been made for the Principal, together with Mrs. Kevan, to visit Latin America in order to conduct a number of Bible conventions, but unfortunately Ernest Kevan's serious illness in 1962 intervened and this tour was never carried out, much to the disappointment of all concerned.

In his own country Ernest Kevan was in considerable demand as a convention speaker. On three occasions he was invited to speak at the Keswick Convention, giving the Bible Readings twice. Among other conventions which he addressed were those at Felixstowe, Llandrindod Wells and Abinger.

Mention must also be made of Ernest Kevan's literary activities. His *magnum opus* was of course, *The Grace of Law*. This was, in fact, the thesis which he submitted successfully for his Ph.D. He loved the Puritans, and in this book he is almost exclusively concerned with their teaching. Reviewing the book, Professor Norman Anderson describes it as 'an eminently fair, meticulous and even exhaustive study—admirably arranged, and with a synopsis at the beginning of each chapter, which not only makes for clarity but also aids review and cross-reference'. The way in which the book is presented is in itself a revelation of the thoroughness and concern for detail which were hallmarks of Ernest Kevan's character. With the Puritans, Ernest Kevan believed that the moral law was adequately revealed to man at creation, and an awareness of it inscribed on his heart. At the Fall, man's knowledge of this law was greatly diminished, and his moral ability to keep it weakened, although neither knowledge of its precepts nor ability to respond to it was wholly lost. The same divine law was crystallised in the Decalogue, which is still binding on men and women today, whether believers or unbelievers. The sinfulness of man is seen not only in his ability to keep this law, but also by his adverse reaction to it. Ernest Kevan rightly believed that the teaching of the Puritans on the law of God was particularly appropriate to the modern situation. In the Foreword which he wrote to his book he said, 'The Puritans stemmed the tide of moral indifference in their day by the use of the Ten Commandments, and it may well be that part of the answer to the modern dilemma is to be found by listening again to the voice of the Puritans, and receiving the truth to which they bore testimony.'

Several of Ernest Kevan's works were first published in the

United States, among them *The Moral Law* and *Salvation*. In the latter book the author begins his study with an enquiry into man's need of salvation, and proceeds to expound the grace of God and the plan by which God fulfils His saving purposes. Writing in the Preface, the author states, 'In its widest sense the Doctrine of Salvation comprehends everything that God has said and done for the purpose of bringing sinful man back to Himself. It touches and is touched by almost every aspect of Christian truth. It is like a golden thread running through all the areas of Christian doctrine and uniting them together.' Ernest Kevan was a contributor to *Baker's Dictionary of Theology*, and wrote a chapter on 'The Principles of Interpretation' for the symposium, *Revelation and the Bible*, edited by Dr. Carl F. H. Henry.

Together with the late Professor F. Davidson and the Rev. A. M. Stibbs, Ernest Kevan served as one of the editors of the *New Bible Commentary*, published by the Inter-Varsity Fellowship in 1953. This volume had been eagerly awaited, and the first printing which consisted of 30,000 copies sold almost overnight. Those responsible for its production sought to combine careful scholarship with respect for the inspiration and essential historical trustworthiness of the text. Ernest Kevan was responsible for the section dealing with the book of Genesis.

It would no doubt surprise some to discover that a man of such profound scholarship could also write very simply for young Christians. In this respect we see him at his best in the volume, *Going On*. This book, which is concisely and clearly written, is aimed to help young converts to make progress in the Christian life. The writer defines the theological terms which he uses, and clearly reveals that he has kept in touch with young people over the years. It is significant that the book of Ernest Kevan's which was published shortly after his death consisted of a series of children's addresses with the title, *Let's Talk*. Ernest Kevan excelled in the art of speaking to children but, unlike some children's addresses, those which he gave were full of biblical content. He could present profound truth in a winsome manner and in such a way that boys and girls held on to his every word. Woven into a number of the addresses are personal incidents relating to the author's own boyhood.

All Ernest Kevan's published works reveal not only his careful scholarship and concern for accuracy, but also his ability to state profound truths lucidly. Furthermore, his writings while revealing his own strong convictions nevertheless are refreshingly free from any vitriolic spirit, for Dr. Kevan was no lover of controversy.

We see, then, that the College Principal was a man who was widely read and who travelled extensively in the service of the gospel. Always, however, his first love was the College which became so closely identified with his name. In every consideration the College came first. He never allowed himself to be diverted from the main purpose to which he believed God had called him. One of Dr. Kevan's great gifts was that of being able to delegate work to others while still retaining overall control himself. He displayed this gift in the various churches that he served, and to a special degree in organising the life and work of the College.

The orderliness of his mind was reflected in the way in which he ran the College. Nothing escaped his notice. Although getting through an enormous amount of work he always appeared to be unruffled and unhurried. His elaborate filing system, which Mrs. Kevan often called 'his toy', was a further indication of his love of order and his attention to detail. His lectures were delivered with remarkable lucidity and clarity. His thoroughness in all that he did was an inspiration to successive generations of students. Many recall with particular delight his lectures on Homiletics and Pastoral Theology. These were given in a more relaxed atmosphere than was possible with lectures which led up to University examinations. On these occasions there was always abundant evidence of 'the human touch'. At times guffaws of laughter could be heard coming from the Lecture Room as Dr. Kevan, with his inimitable wit, spoke of some of the pitfalls facing the young minister.

Ernest Kevan was a great believer in work. On more than one occasion he said to his students, "Man was made for work; he is never happier than when he is doing it." This dictum he exemplified in his own life. Students coming to the College after having taken a course at a University often admitted that they now had to work as they had never worked before. But no one really minded, since the Principal set the pace and himself worked as hard if not harder than any one else. To work in and for the College was his greatest joy. The College was his life; he could not keep away from it, even in vacations. Everything he did, everywhere he spoke, he always had the College in mind.

CHAPTER SEVEN

TRIBUTE TO A GREAT LEADER

In August 1958 the Chairman of the Board, Mr. Philip S. Henman, received from Dr. Kevan a letter in his own handwriting. It stated :

> 'The purpose of this letter is to share with you some unfortunate news that was made known to me by two doctors last week ... I had a severe attack of angina last Wednesday ... Both doctors explain that although with care I might continue to live as full a life as possible, there is the fairly definite certainty that I will not be able to go on as long as might otherwise have been the case. This grave news puts the whole of my life into a new perspective.'

On May 31st 1962, Ernest Kevan had his first really serious illness. It took the form of a coronary thrombosis and necessitated spending five weeks in hospital. His medical advisers did not at the outset expect him to recover. He was taken ill at his home with a sharp pain which he thought was an attack of angina, but he was quickly removed to Hampstead Hospital. Gradually he recovered and, after he left hospital, spent a month recuperating in Bournemouth. He was not able to return to full duties at the College until January 1st 1963, although towards the end of 1962 he did attend some Board and Faculty meetings, and he kept a keen interest in all that was going on. Dr. H. D. McDonald, the Vice-Principal, stepped into the breach and conducted the affairs of the College in the absence of its Principal. At the time of this illness some of his medical advisers recommended that he should retire. If he did so they felt that he had a reasonable expectation of at least a dozen further years of life, whereas if he insisted on carrying on he might reduce that span to a mere two or three years. It ought to be said that not all those who advised him medically shared this view. Ernest Kevan however was one who would want to die in harness, and he was quite sure that as far as he was concerned the right thing was to carry on as soon as his strength allowed him. The Board of Governors went out of their way to try to persuade him to take things more easily, but he found it very difficult to accede to their request. His heart was in the College, and while he was there he felt he must give his full attention to it. In spite of the seriousness of the illness which he had suffered, he was soon back very much where he was before, not only attending the College each day and taking a full part in it, but also preaching in various parts of the country at week-ends. It seemed his recovery had been complete. Events, however, were to prove otherwise, for within a very few years Ernest Kevan was to suffer a further attack from which he did not recover.

Only a week before his fatal illness he presided at the wedding of one of the tutors of the College, Mr. Leslie Allen. Mr. Allen married a former student, Miss Elizabeth Gulliver, and the wedding took place at the village of Helmdon in Northamptonshire. Dr. and Mrs. Kevan called at the home of Mr. H. Carey Oakley and drove him to the wedding. It was a delightfully happy occasion. After the marriage service Dr. Kevan attended the reception and was in one of his humorous moods. Later, he and Mrs. Kevan brought Mr. Carey Oakley back to his home in St. Albans, and stayed with him for a while chatting over a cup of tea. At that time there was no suggestion that within a week Dr. Kevan would be stricken down with an illness which would prove fatal. On Sunday, August 22nd 1965, he preached at his beloved Trinity Road Chapel. His text in the morning was taken from the book of Isaiah, chapter 41, verse 10, while in the evening he preached from St. Mark's Gospel, chapter 2, verse 17. He appeared to be in excellent health, and many who heard his messages on that day remarked on the power with which they were delivered. This of course was vacation time as far as the College was concerned, but even so Dr. Kevan rarely missed being away for a single day from his desk. He was there as usual on Friday, August 27th, and during the afternoon he complained of feeling ill and had severe pain round his heart, which he took to be an attack of angina. He left the College earlier than usual, drove himself home and went straight to bed. The doctor was called, and that evening Dr. Kevan had several serious heart attacks. In the small hours of Saturday, August 28th, he passed into the presence of His Lord and Master. So ended the earthly life of the one who had played a more significant part than any other human being in the formation and development of the London Bible College. He had begun by being a part-time tutor, then became Resident Tutor, and from 1946 served the College as its Principal. It was at the express wish of Mrs. Kevan that I, who had been a close friend of her husband's for many years, conducted the funeral service. This was held on Thursday, September 2nd, in Trinity Road Chapel, which was crowded to overflowing. In spite of the fact that this was the holiday season, many distinguished Christian leaders were present in the congregation, as well as hosts of former students of the College. The Vice-Principal, Dr. McDonald, flew back that very morning from Chicago in order to be present. Brief tributes were paid to Dr. Kevan by the Rev. J. Clement Connell, Director of Studies, and by the Chairman of the Board, Mr. P. S. Henman. The interment was in nearby Wandsworth Cemetery.

On Thursday, October 14th 1965, a great company gathered in the Metropolitan Tabernacle for a Memorial Service which was convened in order to give thanks to God for the life of Dr. Kevan. The College Chairman, Mr. P. S. Henman, conducted the service, and tributes to Dr. Kevan were paid by the Chairman, the Vice-Principal and the Rev. Edmund Heddle, representing former students of the College. The closing address was given by the Rev. John R. W. Stott, Rector of All Souls, Langham Place. Mr. Henman referred to the late Principal as a 'wise master builder'. He said, "Step by step and stone by stone, adhering faithfully to the original plan, he built the London Bible College as we know it today." Mr. Henman drew attention to the fact to which so many others have referred, that Dr. Kevan had a deep personal interest in each member of his staff and every student of the College.

Dr. H. Dermot McDonald, Vice-Principal of the College, pointed out that Dr. Kevan was more than a Principal; he was a friend to all—a brother beloved. The two men had worked together in the happiest association for seventeen years. The Vice-Principal referred to Dr. Kevan as a man of greatness, a man of grace, and a man of the gospel. He was great in knowledge, and was a deep thinker and profound theologian, but he never lost his tremendous sense of being a debtor to mercy alone. The doctrines of Grace were his special delight, for he loved to expound and to explore them. He was essentially a man of the gospel. One of the last things that he said was, "I love to preach the gospel." What he taught in the class-room with conviction he preached in the pulpit with authority.

The Rev. Edmund Heddle, one of the early students at the College, also paid tribute to his former Principal. In the course of his address he said, "He always had time for us, both in College and afterwards. As we went to his room, his 'Come in' was full of genuine pleasure, and though in the midst of a busy schedule of College life there was no sense of rush about the interview; rather, you felt that he was just waiting to see you." His knowledge of each member of the College family was also outstanding. "When he stayed in our homes," said Mr. Heddle, "or dropped in at our Manses in the course of a journey, his conversation would reveal that he remembered us all. He was closely in touch with the events in the church and the members of the family. His prayers continued long after we had left College. He always used to say, 'Once a member of the College, always a member of the College'."

In a closing tribute the Rev. John Stott pointed to three characteristics in Ernest Kevan which called for special commendation. He referred to the strength and stability of his Christian conviction; coupled with this conviction was moral courage comparable with the 16th-century reformers. Yet, as Mr. Stott went on to point out, in the person of Dr. Kevan there was a most unusual combination of strength and gentleness. There was abundance of Christian courtesy. He added, "As Principal of the London Bible College, he was firm and immovable in his evangelical convictions and yet he was as tender as a mother with little children. He could be wonderfully patient with backward, obtuse and unintelligent students; deeply sympathetic with those in trouble and sorrow; and very gracious towards his theological opponents."

Those who spoke at the Memorial Service did so, of course, in a representative capacity. Similar tributes to the memory of Dr. Kevan came from all those who had known him and had been his colleagues over the years.

The Rev. J. H. Stringer, one of the early tutors at the College, has aptly described the College's first Principal as being 'the right man in the right place at the right time'. Miss Margaret Manton, who first came to the College as a student, and later was invited on to the tutorial staff by Dr. Kevan, pays a warm tribute to her former Principal. "Dr. Kevan always made one want to do the best work and be the best in character that was possible. He tolerated no low standards himself, and, while not finding fault in low standards in others except when absolutely necessary, his own example of consistent life, immaculate dress, hard work and sheer integrity set its own standard ... The sovereignty of God dominated his whole life, and somehow his whole life and preaching illustrated this." Like so many others Margaret Manton points out that when he died she felt as though she had lost a close relative. She adds, "In his own home and in the homes of others he was always the same courteous, gentlemanly person, approachable, witty and spiritually-minded, but attractively so."

Another of his colleagues was of course the Secretary of the College, Mr. Donald R. Baker. At the time when the buildings in Marylebone Road seemed totally inadequate to meet the demands of the ever-growing College, the Principal and the Secretary were brought very close together, discussing the future and studying possible plans for the extension of the College, or alternatively looking for a new site for building the College elsewhere. The two men worked together for eight years, and Donald Baker pays this tribute. "Dr. Kevan could be severe but wholly sympathetic. He commanded loyalty from his colleagues, but no one could have been more loyal than he. His capacity for work was tremendous and he expected only a slightly lower standard from everybody else. His personal affection for anybody connected with the College had to be experienced to be appreciated. His gift of language and choice of words delighted his listeners; his occasional humour when relaxed was delightful, but at all times his nearness to the Lord was obvious and his reserves of spiritual strength were given freely to his friends." Mr. Baker was in a position to see what many others have commented upon—the fact that Dr. Kevan was interested in every detail and gave meticulous attention to every aspect of the work, always sharing a concern that everything should be done decently and in good order.

Mr. Timothy J. Buckley seems to have been regarded by Dr.

Kevan as a spiritual son. Mr. Buckley joined the staff of the College in 1950, as Extension Secretary, and was later invited by the Principal to attend meetings of the tutorial staff. He recalls many happy occasions when he and his family enjoyed the company of Dr. and Mrs. Kevan. A common interest in and love for music brought the two families close together. Mr. Buckley remarks on the great sense of humour which Dr. Kevan had, and of the way in which children were specially attracted to him. Towards the end of his life when Dr. Kevan was advised to take up some relaxing hobby, he determined he would learn to play the cello. Within six months, due to his tenacity of purpose and self-discipline, he was able to play the instrument reasonably well. Mr. Buckley recalls one occasion when the College Principal played alongside young Stephen Buckley, then aged six, in the parish hall of Dagenham. Dr. Kevan was not in the least perturbed by the fact that at that time Stephen could play as well as he could!

It has only been possible to quote from a few of the letters received from those who had worked alongside Dr. Kevan. All his colleagues said much the same, for they all loved and admired him greatly. They all recognised in him a true man of God endowed to an unusual degree with the spirit of wisdom and understanding. As Dr. McDonald pointed out, "as long as the London Bible College stands at the corner of the road in Marylebone, or anywhere else, the name of its first Principal will not die. He was called to take over the work when the College was a struggling infant. Others had been the midwife bringing it to birth, but he was called to nurse it and to see to its development. And he did his work with commensurate skill and superb effectiveness."

Tributes poured into the College from many different quarters when the news of Dr. Kevan's death became generally known. In this chapter, we must content ourselves with but one—that of the Rev. Dr. G. R. Beasley-Murray, Principal of Spurgeon's College. "Dr. Kevan's passing is an incalculable loss to the whole Christian Church . . . one of the most gracious men on earth who must have been held not only in esteem but in affection by a multitude."

CHAPTER EIGHT

THROUGH STUDENT EYES

From the many letters sent by former students, which arrived at the College following the announcement of Dr. Kevan's death, one gains the impression that the first Principal of the College had made a lasting impression on those who had passed through his hands. In the tributes which were paid to him, certain characteristics were singled out and referred to in letter after letter.

There was, for example, repeated reference to his pastoral concern. Several students pointed out that they were impressed by the fact that he was never too busy to see them and hear them as individuals. 'What a wonderful interest he had in everyone and their problems. He was a real pastor', wrote Mr. Stuart Aldis. David Appavoo, an Indian student who had been at the College, wrote, 'I had come to love him and to honour him. In all my problems he had an interest and helpful suggestion and prayerful remembrance. I always turned to him as a son would turn to his father.' 'Not only a lecturer but a friend', wrote another. Vivienne Stacey, a missionary now serving in West Pakistan with the Bible and Medical Missionary Fellowship, wrote, 'His deep personal interest in his thousand and one old students never ceased to cause me to wonder. He was my ideal for a College Principal.'

Another characteristic in the life of Dr. Kevan which was frequently mentioned was his orderliness and attention to detail. Different students remarked on the clarity of thought and lucidity of his lectures. Several mentioned his filing system, to which we have already referred and which became almost legendary among students of the College.

In their letters not a few students recalled various humorous incidents which took place during their time at College and in which the Principal played some part. One incident related to the very early days in the old building at 19 Marylebone Road when Dr. and Mrs. Kevan lived on the premises. Apparently the Principal was having a bath. Some rather impatient student who was anxious to have a bath himself felt that this particular bathroom had been occupied for rather a long time. He was told that it was the Principal who was occupying it, but he was incredulous. He walked up to the bathroom door, knocked loudly on it and shouted, "How long are you going to be, Ernie?" One can imagine his horror when after a slight pause a very dignified voice answered from within, "I shall not be long." Needless to say, the student in question was covered in confusion, although no subsequent reference was made to the incident. Dr. Kevan always enjoyed the fun of the annual Christmas concert, when light-hearted references were often made to him and to his colleagues. He particularly enjoyed a scene on one occasion, which purported to depict his 'visit to the Pope'.

The Principal was always immaculately dressed, and in his lectures on Pastoral Theology he invariably stressed the need to be neat and tidy in appearance. When he was dilating on this theme at some length on one particular occasion, there was a white cotton hanging from the hem of his jacket. Greatly daring, a lady student drew his attention to this. He joined heartily in the laughter at his expense which followed. Some time later, the student felt somewhat conscience stricken at the line which she had taken. The next day she approached Dr. Kevan as he stood in the entrance hall, thinking that this would be a fitting opportunity to apologise to him. However, before she could open her mouth he came towards her and said, "Miss Manton, just look me over before I go into Chapel, will you, please?"

Some students commented on other aspects of their late Principal's character. Ernest Kevan was a strong disciplinarian. He belonged to 'the old school'. He was a stickler for seeing that all things were done 'decently and in order'. He could tolerate neither slovenliness nor unpunctuality. Even when there was a transport strike which virtually paralysed London, he had little sympathy with those who arrived late at College. There were occasions when certain students resented being treated, as they felt, like children, but Ernest Kevan's sole aim was to impress upon those who came to the College the need for maintaining the dignity of the pastoral office. There was no vestige of pride in him as a man, but he rightly believed that the office should be duly respected. One of the students who came to the College from abroad, John Madsen of Copenhagen, writes, 'The general impression he created among the students was one of respect and confidence. His very person and appearance caused us to respect him. Yet we quickly found out that a tender and loving heart beat beneath his worthy appearance.'

Another impression which Dr. Kevan left on his students was that of fair-mindedness. Although he himself had a strong Strict Baptist background, he never overlooked the fact that he was the Principal of an interdenominational college, and took fully into consideration the differing points of view held by evangelical Christians on a number of issues. When dealing with such controversial matters as baptism, church order or the interpretation of prophecy, he would be scrupulously fair in putting forth the various points of view and interpretations, while at the same time not hiding his personal convictions. He never took the opportunity of 'getting at' those with whom he disagreed. The story is told of one student who came to the College with strong convictions about believer's baptism, but who after listening to Dr. Kevan's presentation of the case for infant baptism became an Anglican!

One of Dr. Kevan's outstanding characteristics was his intense interest in the old students of the College. During their time at the College students were always addressed by the Principal with strict formality as 'Mr.' or 'Miss', but from the day that they left he invariably used their Christian names. A new and intimate relationship started, which continued from that moment onwards. To hundreds and hundreds of old students he remained right up to his death a true 'father in God'. Through the years, Dr. and Mrs. Kevan were the beloved host and hostess at the annual gatherings of the Old Students' Association. He showed an intense interest in every former student. He could never easily resist the request of an old student to speak at an anniversary. Missionaries on furlough would invariably make their way to his study and seek his counsel. Men with problems in their pastorates would turn to him for advice. He was personally interested in the home and family life of his former students. He would take pains to remember the names of their children when he visited their homes. Little wonder that his death was an occasion for personal sorrow on the part of all who had known him and loved. him. One student wrote, 'I must confess the sense of loss that I experienced with the knowledge of the passing of our beloved Principal was greater than I dreamed possible.' Another wrote, 'I myself felt numbed throughout the remainder of the day after I heard the news of his homecall, and I thought that never again could I turn to one to whom I often turned and had never failed to receive the help and guidance that I needed.' 'The Lord blessed us with a great pastor and leader,' wrote yet another. Many old students said that they could not picture the College without him. As far as they were concerned, he was the College. In her sorrow Mrs. Kevan was deeply touched by the volume of letters which she personally received, each expressing appreciation and gratitude for the ministry of her husband. Acknowledging these tributes she wrote, 'It is wonderful to know that my dear husband was so beloved. It is also a great comfort to know of those who have been blessed through his ministry. This would be his crowning joy.'

CHAPTER NINE

'THE FATHER OF HIS PEOPLE'

It is recorded that Oliver Cromwell addressed the artist who had been commissioned to paint his portrait thus: "Mr. Lely, I desire you would use all your skill to paint my picture truly like me and not flatter me at all; but remark all these roughnesses, pimples, warts and everything as you see me, otherwise I'll never pay a farthing for it." Where warts exist, the artist, if he is to produce a true likeness, is bound to reproduce them. Such 'warts' as there may have been in the character of Ernest Kevan were certainly not easily detectable. He combined so very many good qualities that one finds it extremely difficult to recall any faults or failings that he may have had. It would be true to say, however, that those who did not know him well often gained a false impression of him. His presence seemed to some on first acquaintance to be slightly forbidding. His concern for dignity made him appear somewhat austere and perhaps not readily approachable.

In common with all men in public life Ernest Kevan had his critics. There were those who suggested that he placed too much emphasis on academic attainment. There were others who felt that he was so devoted to the interests of the College that he could take little real interest in any other form of Christian work. Some hinted that he produced at the College a generation of 'little Kevans', men who had moulded themselves slavishly on his own life and character. Ernest Kevan was well aware of these and other criticisms that were made, but he was not resentful. At the same time, he was always ready to take up the cudgels on behalf of the College when he felt this to be necessary. He was perhaps particularly troubled by the accusation made in some quarters that the London Bible College was not a missionary training college. This, he claimed, was far from the truth. It was largely to scotch such accusations that he advised the appointment of the Rev. John Savage as Director of Missionary Studies. In a letter to John Savage, written in 1954, Ernest Kevan sums up his own approach to the subject:

'It is our conviction that the primary elements of missionary training are found in the study of the Bible and of Christian truth. This, after all, is what it is that the missionary has to take to the people, and all other purely "technical" and "manual" subjects are more easily learned on the mission field itself and under the guidance of a superior missionary. We do feel, however, that general instruction in the history of Christian missions, the knowledge of other religions, and the most up-to-date missionary methods is something that needs to be given in student days.'

Ernest Kevan was anxious that every student in the College, whatever his or her future was to be, should have a missionary vision, and he went out of his way to fulfil this ideal. The realities of the missionary situation in India which he saw for himself increased, if anything, his concern for the spiritual calibre of prospective missionaries.

Ernest Kevan came under fire from certain quarters because of his interpretation of prophecy. He was an a-millennialist, in other words he did not believe in a literal millennium, a thousand year period of earthly bliss following the second advent of Christ. A-millennialism rests on a symbolic interpretation of the 20th chapter of the Book of Revelation. Those who share this view believe that the second advent of Christ will synchronise with the resurrection of the wicked and the last judgment. The present earth will pass away and give place to a new heaven and a new earth. It is surprising how bitter some students of prophecy can be towards those whose views do not coincide with their own. A special series of articles appeared in one magazine attacking Dr. Kevan and the position which he held. Copies of the articles were sent to him, but he did not attempt to reply or defend himself. He refused to be drawn into controversy. He hated it.

Ernest Kevan has been described as a fundamentally shy man. While he was greatly respected by very many people, he did not find it easy to make close friends. There was a certain diffidence about him, and he was by nature extremely sensitive and tenderhearted. At the same time, he was a man of strong character. He went fearlessly ahead when he was sure that he was in the line of the divine will. On such occasions, nothing could daunt him. He was, in fact, something of an autocrat. One who knew him well has said, "Quite unwittingly while he sought counsel of his colleagues, and really paid attention to what they had to say, his mind was often quite clearly made up, and he pressed on like a ship under full sail." An autocrat maybe, but certainly a 'benevolent' despot.

Of coures, as so many remarked, he was also a born organiser. His genuine concern was that in everything connected with God's work the highest possible standards should be maintained. He did not mind admitting that he warmed to a certain amount of ceremonialism. Good-humouredly, some of his friends have suggested he might have made a good Anglo-Catholic. He did have a 'high' doctrine of the Church, and particularly of the sacred office of preaching the Word.

For some, the memory of this man of God will remain fragrant all their lives as being one they were privileged to know as a beloved pastor for in each of his churches he was held in the highest esteem and greatest affection by his people. Almost a thousand young men and women look back upon him as a true father in God, a college principal who was to them the embodiment of all that a minister of the gospel should be, and whose example they will always seek to emulate. For his colleagues on the staff of the London Bible College, the memory will be of a man gifted with gracious leadership who had a real concern for those who worked with him, for their families as well as for themselves, and who was utterly devoted to the task to which God had called him. In the eyes of the gracious lady who was his helpmeet for so many years, Ernest Kevan's memory will ever be that of a loving and devoted husband from whose never-failing courtesies many other husbands might well learn a lesson.

Ultimately, there can be only one explanation of such a life— the grace of God. At the same time, we do well to acknowledge those factors which God used in moulding this man's life—an upbringing in a godly home, the cultivation of habits of strong self-discipline, a willingness to devote himself wholly to the task to which he had been called, and the tender sympathy of a beloved helpmeet.

One might conclude this brief biography with words which Dr. Kevan delighted to quote in the pulpit, always with a radiant expression on his face as he did so—

> *O think!*
> *To step on shore,*
> *And that shore heaven!*
> *To take hold of a Hand,*
> *And that God's Hand!*
> *To breath a new air,*
> *And feel it celestial air;*
>
> *To feel invigorated,*
> *And know it immortality!*
> *O think!*
> *To pass from the storm and the tempest*
> *To one unbroken calm!*
> *To wake up,*
> *And find it—GLORY.*

EPILOGUE

I have written of Dr. Kevan's fruitful ministry both in the churches which he served and as Principal of the London Bible College. It is fitting that the last word should be his. Although originally written at the time when the College was in process of formation, his words of advice to those contemplating training for full-time Christian service are as relevant now as they were then. I therefore pass them on in the prayerful hope that they may be of help to at least some of those who read them.

AM I READY FOR TRAINING?

This is a question which everyone ought to ask himself before applying for admission to a training college in connection with Christian service. Perhaps your immediate inward response is, "Do I not go to the college or institute to be prepared? Have I not just to present myself, and then like a piece of soft clay offer myself to be shaped and moulded?" The answer to your question is "No!" Training is not passive but active. You will receive from a training course only as much benefit as you have fitted yourself to take. The value of entering into full-time training is not merely in what the tutors are able to do for you, but what they are able to help you to do for yourself. It will not do, therefore, just to fill in a form of application, and then come 'to be trained'. You need to prepare yourself for entry into a college, whether the academic standards of that college be high or low; whether there be a preliminary entrance examination or not.

I propose to mention six specific points in connection with which you should begin to prepare yourself if you desire to embark upon full-time training.

1. Spiritual preparation

By spiritual preparation I mean that you should know that you are doing God's will. There is no advantage in doing anything, however good in itself, unless you are in the line of God's purpose for your life. Ask yourself this question: "Why am I proposing to enter upon full-time training?" No college exists just to give 'luxury cruises in learning' to men and women who think they can afford it. Such students are capable of becoming a real hindrance in the life of a college. Before you think of applying for admission to a Bible or missionary college, be sure that you know something of God's will for you. You may not know just where He wants you to serve Him; but you must have the Holy Spirit's conviction wrought within you that, like Paul of old, you have been 'separated unto the gospel' (Romans 1.1).

It is important, however, to remember that having failed in business life does not constitute a qualification for entering the ministry! There are some who, because they have made a bad job of everything else, feel that the Lord is calling them into the ministry. You may take it as a fairly safe rule that if you are no good at your present employment you will be no good in the ministry. Try to read C. H. Spurgeon's lecture to his students on 'The Call to the Ministry'.

2. Mental preparation

How long is it since you left school? How have you been occupied since you left school? These are important questions for you to consider. I know a young man who had been serving in a draper's shop for ten years after he left school, and then God led him to prepare for the ministry. He was truly called of God to this; but, owing to the habits of mind which he had formed during ten years behind the draper's counter, he found it very hard going for the first two terms in the college. He had a perpetual headache for nearly six months. It is highly important that, if you have been accepted by a college, you should prepare yourself by gradual increase of mental effort beforehand. This is necessary, whatever may be the academic standards of the college that you propose to enter. Some colleges have an entrance examination for which you must work. This is useful in giving guidance to the college, but it is even more valuable for your own mind. You should have enough respect for learning, and for the college, to compel you to make yourself as worthy as possible for the trouble that the principal and tutors will take over you.

To be concrete, if you desire to present yourself as an applicant for admission to a college, you must make yourself familiar with the general contents of the Bible. The least you must do is to read the Bible through. If you will not study at home, you certainly will not study at college. Character and mental discipline are the things that count in training.

3. Theological preparation

An even balance is required in regard to theological opinions. The mind needs to be established in the foundational things, but to be nicely poised with regard to those aspects of doctrine upon which legitimate difference of judgment exists. Your theological preparation should therefore be of the sort that *inquires*. You will need to acquire the open mind for truth, even if it happens to be different from the ideas that you may have previously conceived. Theological bigotry is the greatest handicap from which you can possibly suffer. I think it was Oliver Wendell Holmes who said the mind of a bigot is like the pupil of the eye : the greater the light shining upon it the more it closes up. Your theological preparation for entry into a Bible college is not that of fixed and immovable opinions or prejudices, but that of general familiarity with the field of theological thought.

No better preparation in this connection can be provided than by reading through some book of systematic theology. Never mind if you do not grasp everything there : indeed, it will be as well to reserve judgment on all controversial subjects at this preliminary stage of your studies. You are just opening your eyes and looking at the delectable country through which you will later have to travel with much labour. As a suggestion, I would recommend you to read Rev. T. C. Hammond's handbook, *In Understanding Be Men*.

4. Practical preparation

One of the first questions you will be asked by an interviewing committee when you apply to enter a training college will be, "What Christian service are you now rendering?" We learn by doing; and it is in the practical work of Sunday school or mission that most of our lessons are learned. Those desiring to enter the preaching ministry must prove themselves in acceptable preaching. Colleges have no use for ornaments: and it is the men and women who by consistent and continued service can show that they mean business who are most likely to gain admission. If you have never done any Sunday school teaching, or open-air preaching, or some other similar form of gospel service you are not properly 'prepared' for entry into a training institution.

Do all that you can, but be careful not to attempt forms of service for which you are obviously not fitted. Use your judgment in these matters. If you find you do not 'get on' at all in either preaching or teaching then you will be well advised to stop and think again before you enter a Bible or missionary college. This practical preparation is all-important.

Remember, too, in this respect, that the consensus of opinion among the people of God is one of the best forms of guidance concerning your practical fitness for special training. Seek the counsel of your minister in this matter: he will very largely be able to present to you the mind of the church concerning your practical abilities.

5. Financial preparation

Little need be said about this, for it is so obvious. You must be in a position to pay whatever fees are required by the authorities of the college you desire to enter. You should find out exactly what is involved in this way. Financial embarrassment can be a great mental burden. While it is true that God calls upon us to live a life of faith, He has also given us sound judgment, and we must exercise this. All this means in brief that if you really feel called to full-time training you will save up for it.

6. Devotional preparation

This is not last because it is least important: nor yet is it last because it is more important. It is here just because something had to be last. All the aspects of preparation of which we have been thinking must be borne in mind proportionately and according to your individual needs. If you are more particularly deficient on any one point, then it may be you must pay special attention in that direction. Keep a balanced view of life all through.

Devotional preparation is extremely important, however; and

by this I mean the maintenance of your own spiritual glow. Even in a preparatory period it is so easy to become absorbed in theology or in practical service that you leave the soil of your own soul untilled and unwatered. The wise preparation for entry into a Bible or missionary college is to foster your own spiritual life. Those learn most who love most : and the more we love God and His Truth the more apt we shall become in studying it, and the more sensitive we shall be to what the Spirit is teaching us in the Holy Scripture. Remember that intellectual insight depends very largely upon spiritual perception.